In This Universe

Meytav Bayin

BookLeaf Publishing

India | USA | UK

Presentation by *BookLeaf Publishing*

Web: www.bookleafpub.com

E-mail: info@bookleafpub.com

ISBN : 9789357448789

First edition 2021

DEDICATION

I dedicate this book to God, for continuously giving me another day to push myself and prove myself. Thank you for the endless calm and clarity You give me, and for always guiding me in the right direction. Your protection is my superpower.

ACKNOWLEDGEMENT

A huge thank you to my parents, Jack and Iris for the endless love and support, and for always being by my side. You have taught me how to love both myself and the world around me, so that I could continue waking up with a smile on my face.
Thank you for motivating me to turn all of my dreams into reality. Your belief in me is what keeps me going.

Building

There is a misconception
That being torn down
Means we are at our lowest.
But everyone knows
That in order to build a stable structure
Upwards
There has to be a
Strong foundation.
And that has to start at
Ground Level.

Your Blossom

To want what another has
Bought
Is to dismiss
What you have
Blossomed.

Superpower

IF YOU LIKE THE FEELING
OF DOING SOMETHING
THAT MOST PEOPLE
CANNOT DO
Start by loving yourself.
Most people don't know how.

Thank You

At the end of the day,
No matter what,
Thank you God.
Even when it is the
Hardest thing to say.
I know you
Saved me
From something
Way worse
Along the way.

Full Potential

I am sorry for questioning
Your plans for me.
Maybe I am scared,
Scared of how much
Everything will change
When I reach my full
Potential.

Good Enough

Maybe it was
Never about
Being good enough,
But being in a
Crowd that makes you feel
Good.
And that's enough.

Reality

I had a crush on a
Dream.
But that meant having
To walk around
With my eyes closed.
Blinded.
Stumbling.
Opening them,
Meant seeing
That reality,
Was much
Brighter.

Heard by You

With millions of people
Screaming
Make sure your voice is the one
That stands out.
There is no shame
In asking for
Exactly what you want.
That is when God listens.

Rapunzel

Finally understanding Rapunzel as an adult
Meant knowing
That she was never
Stuck in a tower.
She was just afraid
To ever come down.
And in reality,
Nobody can save you
From the fear in your own
Mind.

In Awe of You

Have you ever wondered
Whether the
Awe you hold
While looking at the
Stars
Is the same
Awe
Reflected
Back at
You
From the
Entire Universe?

The Sun

You are the
Sun.
Even when it is cloudy,
And it cannot be seen,
I know the sun exists,
And it is always there.
Just as You are.

Entryway

"Thank you for entering my life God."
        ~ "Thank you for letting me in."
The door was always open
I just didn't know
That I was the one
Blocking the entrance.

Colorblind

Growing up
Often feels like
The world has been adjusted to
Grayscale.
Completely leached of all
Color and excitement.
Yet maybe,
The world does not
Lose its color as we get older,
Maybe we just become
Colorblind.
And with the right glasses,
We too can see that
Color again
From a
Child's perspective.

By My Side

Everybody wants someone that will
Fight for them
And
Not let them go.
The kind of person
That no matter what happens,
Tells them
"I am not giving up on us"
The kind of person that
Tells them
"We are too important"
The kind that tells them
"I believe in us"
But over time,
I realized,
That I've been looking in the wrong places
Been asking the
Wrong people
Because the only one that has told me
"I'll always be here"
Was God.

Best Views

The views are always
Better
Up here.
And not because I
Have surpassed
Everyone else,
But to see how far I've come.
And regardless,
There is more of a
Strain
Having to look up
To all the heights I
Could have reached,
But didn't.

Thought Process

Humanity's greatest
Flaw
Is actually a
Thought process.
One that
Constantly views life
As the
Cup half empty.
Always searching
For what is missing.
And never stopping
To appreciate
All that
Already exists.
The problem that
Most people do not understand,
Is that the ultimate recipe
For lack
Is a loss of appreciation
For one's current
Abundance.

Message from Above

"When you love yourself,
You are also loving Me,
Because I am a part of your soul.
And with you,
I am a huge part of your soul.
So when you love yourself,
You are also loving
Everything that I have given you
And appreciating everything
About us both."

-God

Pixie Dust

It is said
That our
Destiny
Has already been
Written in the stars.
The cosmos.
And maybe it's because
That is how we all started out.
Pixie dust
Floating in absolute
Darkness.
Then we grew and formed
A whole Universe.
Creating magic.

P.S - You are magic.

First Kiss

Maybe having a
First kiss
With the cold night sky
Made me forget
About the upcoming
Sunrise.
> And I always liked the warmth more
than the chill.

Fork in the Road

When there is a
Fork in the road
Do not fear.
As there are no
Wrong turns
When God is near.

Inner Child

I want to dedicate this one to your soul
And your inner child who misses you dearly
And looks at you with such pride and
Unconditional love.
The kind you no longer know how to provide -
For yourself.
That inner child has spent countless nights
praying to be
Everything that you already are.
Waiting on the day to finally step into the shoes
Of the grown up version of themselves.
Standing tall,
Knowing so much,
Having so many more opportunities.
Being more alive than ever before.
That inner child does not understand
What went wrong along the way,
And why the night time always makes you cry,
While the morning sun
Only reminds you that you have to keep
pretending.
Maybe you thought that growing up
Means your inner child no longer exists,
But they never grow old,
And they see through your eyes -

Only from a different perspective
One where there is always more light than dark
One where there is beauty in every flaw
One where there is a reason to smile at every
moment
That inner child misses you,
And wants you back.
So please listen to what they have to say.
They'll take it from here.